OPHELIAC

OPHELIAC

Poems

EMMA SLOAN

BLACK LAWRENCE PRESS

Black Lawrence Press

Executive Editor: Diane Goettel
Chapbook Editor: Lisa Fay Coutley
Book Cover and Interior Design: Zoe Norvell

ISBN: 978-1-62557-150-2

Published 2024 by Black Lawrence Press.
Printed in the United States.

Table of Contents

"This was always going to happen.
She's been dead since the beginning."

-ORESTES

I

Opheliac

In Steubenville,
Ophelia claws her way up
through the duckweed again.

Look at her just standing there,
John says. Eric tosses
a football into the air and laughs,
tight-lipped,
the beehive of last weekend
rattling loose behind his molars.

Yesterday,
when Eric went to the river
to choke on the word *Sorry* '
'til his tongue went soft,
she sank back into the deep blue
until there was only the mirror
of her dead-deer eyes.

Now, the cheerleaders are filing out
in rows of three. The firelight slides
a palm up the back of their skirts,
the flames red as Ophelia's mouth
gaping, red as her dress hunched
on Eric's basement floor.

There are better things to look at,
he says.

Creation Myth

1.

Let's say–for argument's sake–
that we managed to pour the dead girl
back into her body.
Let's say–because the story's better this way;
makes it an allegory, makes it have meaning–
that we pieced her back together   through photographs,
through peonies,
through our recollections and half-lies
of why last August ended up
on the cutting room floor.

2.

Ophelia on the bus. Ophelia in the back of the class.
Ophelia's hair dripping dogwood
onto the road, onto the school sidewalk, onto the tiles
of the boys' bathroom.

Fennels for fingertips. Lilies for legs. The pastor calls it

witchcraft at Sunday sermon,

hands white-knuckled as the rhythmic rain from her dress

runs in rivulets between the pews. Eric murmurs, later,

that he hears it outside against his windows

even on clear nights.

3.

All we know with certainty is that, on that summer night,

she was plied with alcohol at a party and woke up more river

than girl. After all, what is a ghost other than something dead

that doesn't know it's dead? Like the unfortunate souls

that the Greek gods once turned to nymphs

in their mercy, Ophelia flowered up

from that sandy bank, donning the dress

we last saw her in.

Hiraeth

Telling this story is me drowning, open-mouthed,
just for the chance to say her name again.

Where does it start?
At any point that I'm not in it.
At any point that I can act
like I didn't know her,
like I don't still drop books
into the Ohio River
so that she has something to read.

Well, we can begin at love.
It's bookmarked.
It's a love like a lacing of the fingers,
like a quick squeeze of the hands.

You know it. You were in it too, once.
Love like it is before it turns sour,
before it turns violent,
before it's his fist as a vise
around the back of her throat,
dragging her loose-limbed
across the coarse face of the carpet
until the memories of them
intertwined on the bus
(the bed, the park bench)
lie in shreds
beneath bare feet.

Somehow, she said to me, once,
he's still the first person I think of
when something good happens.
I still want to call the old him to say,
"You wouldn't believe
what you said to me today."

Only the dead stay in love and 17 forever.
The rest of us have anger to make us stand,
make us walk.
They say the best revenge is living well,
but I'm worried that I'll spend my whole life
seeking a glimpse of you in my rearview mirror.

I didn't know he felt that way.
Her voice is as soft
as a bubbling brook.
Even after he held my head under, I still didn't understand.

Girl Tongue

no more breaking in the word *sorry* 'til it's tired, no more only rearing when tread on, no more gunshot-soft one-night stands, no more hoarding words like sharp things during a manic episode, no more repurposing your throat for vomiting, no more *maybe he's not guilty, he seemed like a nice kid*, no more scraping your tongue blood-raw in the shower, no more faux smiles in the courtroom, *no more no more no more no more* no more girl tongue, pry it out with nail clippers, flush it down the toilet like your childhood fish, sprout a replacement that's more cobra than garden snake.

The Night After, I Have a Dream, and In It–

She's slinging the rope swing
back onto its branch
like a tongue retracting, like a kiss
rewinding,
erasing itself.

This is an ending, of sorts;
maybe the best kind
of ending we could have asked for,
what with the morning sun
slipping through the oak leaves
like something forgotten,

what with her boots steeped in the river,
the slow turn of her head,
and the way she's smiling like how people
only smile in dreams
before they turn sour,
before they rot and fall to the ground

like the apples in last night's nightmare,

exploding into blood

when they hit the roots

of the oak trees.

This is a reel of film

on the cutting room floor;

this is the scene of her saying See you tomorrow,

and receding into the shrubbery with the light and the wind cascading

through her ropes of brown hair. This is her counting to ten,

the rope swing curling back

onto the forest floor. It's the director's cut; it's her blood arcing over the sand

of the bank below; it's her laughter ringing through the trees

until I wake.

II

Hay Fever Season

the dread of hay fever season:
the anticipation that bleeds
the chalk from the football field
and into the Ohio River,
makes it run swifter, blacker,
makes it froth with a hunger
that's not its own.

it's the slow-creeping trepidation
that skulks through town
like white clover.
it's the pollen that cloaks
the trees, the traffic lights.

bubblegum lips pop around
the latest slab of gossip; the girls
carve it with steak knives and eat
with their fingers.
the boys have their heads bowed,
necks limp with sun stroke,
the crests on their jerseys
flashing crimson under the midday sun.

listen, listen.
something in this town's
not right.

Serendipity

It's Tuesday,
and we're skipping fourth period
to stuff sage
into mason jars.

When she says,
I am so tired of boys going
"I'll kill him,"
because they never follow through,

I tip my head back,
and my laughter is like glass
and gravel
grinding into the soft give
of my throat.

Well, I'm *not a boy.*

When John's motorbike
careens into the quarry
the dusk before football tryouts,
the school is flooded
with silence.

I get detention
for flouncing down the A-wing,
all teeth,
a string of soot-blackened sage
clenched in one fist.

Onomatology

Ophelia is Greek. It means *aid*, or *help*.

What are we left with after a myth,

          other than the name?
                    Not Ophelia orating from her throne
of underwater volcanoes;

          not Ophelia as the flowers under your feet;
                    not Ophelia as the river's ripples,
          its spray dissolving   into stars.

It's less that I'm still in love with you

                    and more that I tie your memory
          to a time in my life where every door
was thrown open,

                    beckoning in every possibility.

I am Hamlet. I am Ophelia.

          I am my best friend   knee-deep
in the middle of this story,

                                        but I don't want to drink from it.

          (I would do anything for you   except stay.)

Twist the Kaleidoscope Again

There are so many iterations of the same memory, a single one splintering into a thousand as though it's been sifted through a kaleidoscope, but it goes something like *I didn't want to go, but it was time to leave* or *you were gone before I'd even realized you'd chosen to say goodbye* or *you can pull someone out of a burning building, but what if they're the thing that's on fire?*

I still see you as whisper-shy by the riverside, backlit by an endless summer afternoon, instead of snarling in the spring-time– dizzy with delusion, frantically pulling the puzzle pieces of our lives apart until all that's left are the jagged pieces you've fashioned yourself–

and there is no how-to guide on grief, but I twist the kaleidoscope until there's something that resembles seeing you one last time *(I didn't)* by the water where we first walked *(there wasn't)* so that you could hear that I hoped you would be okay *(you weren't).*

Eat Your Teeth First

—no, swallow
with amaretto and coke,
no chewing.

dip your fingers in relish,
your tongue in steak sauce.
keep your legs for running,
your feet as hands
to feel fresh laundry,
stalks of grass,
the wet concrete
that pillows your head
after your tenth shot.

your mom bangs
on the bathroom door
while you're carving out
your left hip bone,
sneaking in a bite
before dinner.

III

Home

There's a type of hauntedness
that's architectural.

In the dream Eric can't talk about,
the kitchen is carved in two.
His father is pressing a gleaming knife edge
into his open palm, eyes marbled with liquor.
The ceiling is on fire.
The floor is flooded with swamp.

Sure, you moved out,
John says,
taking a long drag
of their shared cigarette,
but what does it matter?
You'll always be there,
in that house.

When he meets Ophelia,
it feels like the chance
to build something new.
To rip his foundations out
at the roots.
To give himself new windows,
a new coat of paint.

Instead, the past is a corridor
he can't stop waking up in.
The house is always on fire.
Every confession
is an apology.

Fermata

the morning light jumps like carp between the trees. eight paces away, the abandoned water reservoir juts up through the treetops, sodden with light. vines strain towards the sun. the riverbank stretches out before it, not in waiting but in the sleep that comes after the waiting has been in vain. icicles of rust drip from its barbed wire gate.

there are grooves there, in the panels that flank either side of the gate; ghosts of our converse, our loafers, of the slick-soled boots you wore on our first attempt to hoist each other over to the roof, onto the expanse of broken beer bottles and abandoned pizza boxes and graffiti rubbed away by rain. the ghost of our laughter bubbles up from the concrete like the froth of a faraway river. there are shadows of our first meteor shower, our haloes of tea lights; afterimages of polaroid flashes and flashlights slicing white through darkness, your bare feet skimming the river as the rope swing arcs overhead. memories trapped in time like echoes, still rebounding off the surrounding trees.

1992

Magic has always existed here.
By August, Granddad says,
the cicadas had clustered
on every windowpane in town.
Like shifting kaleidoscopes of black,
he says:
their whine drilled through the glass,
made the whole town rumble
from its roots to its streetlights.
An unlubricated sound,
he says—
a sound that vibrates through
your skull, your soles,
the backs of your teeth.

Daylight didn't exist for five days
back in '92:
the cicadas poured like oil onto the streets,
filled in the cracks in the cobblestone,
blotted out the sun
like storm clouds thrumming
with thunder.

What happened next, Granddad?

They were coming into houses, next.
Seeping through door frames;
spilling into basements.
And the townsfolk, with our mosquito-net visors,
the cicadas' whine pounding through us

like a second heartbeat,
went to the town square
and flicked open the lighters
in our hands.
Eight thousand eyes
turned on us.

Prelude

Every morning, the sun's red spill
slips back behind the mountaintops.
Every morning, the worn soles
of Ophelia's feet skid in reverse
up the gravel, the river ahead
receding, waiting for its time.

The twist of her body towards mine
—an afterthought, the pre-morning
light looping loose around the arch
of her throat—lasts longer every time
that we are here in these woods,
at this river, at this rope swing.

Her smile rewinds. *Your turn*,
she says, the words buoyed
with the joy of not knowing.
The rope is white as bone
in her hands.

You'd think this would start
with a suicide note, a broken nose,
a threat that any girl who loves girls
is a dead girl, but it doesn't.
It starts with a rope in her hand
and a smile in her eyes
and my chest bumping
like a dryer with shoes in it.

I wave my hand in a silent
Tomorrow, but there is
no tomorrow.
Every day is this day, on this hill.
The sun rings the horizon, swollen
like a snakebite.
Crows startle from the treetops
in reverse.

EMMA SLOAN is a poet, short fiction author, and journalist with works published across 300+ international digital and print publications—including, but not limited to, *The Writer Magazine*, *The Vancouver Island Poetry Collective*, *Her Umbrella Magazine*, *Alopecia UK*, and *LandLocked Literary Journal*. She is the author of "Foxglove" (*Chapter House*, 2022). As a Writing and Publishing graduate of the University of Victoria in British Columbia, Canada, Emma works as a professional copywriter and content writer in a multitude of industries. Her creative writing orbits around the intersection between modern mythology and grief. Her chapbook *Opheliac* was named a runner-up in the Black River Chapbook Competition and was published by Black Lawrence Press in fall 2024.